Rosalyn Sussman Yalow

Published in the United States of America by Cherry Lake Publishing
Ann Arbor, Michigan
www.cherrylakepublishing.com

Content Adviser: Ryan Emery Hughes, Doctoral Student, School of Education, University of Michigan
Reading Adviser: Marla Conn MS, Ed., Literacy specialist, Read-Ability, Inc.
Book Design: Jennifer Wahi
Illustrator: Jeff Bane

Photo Credits: © UTBP/Shutterstock, 5; © fortovik/Shutterstock, 7; © Everett Collection / Alamy Stock Photo, 9; © Everett Historical/Shutterstock, 11; © Marguerite T. Hays, 13; © U.S. Department of Veterans Affairs, 15; © ZUMA Press, Inc. / Alamy Stock Photo, 17, 22; © Keystone Pictures USA / Alamy Stock Photo, 19, 23; © Keystone Pictures USA / Alamy Stock Photo, 21; Cover, 6, 10, 16, Jeff Bane; Various frames throughout, © Shutterstock Images

Library of Congress Cataloging-in-Publication Data

Names: Loh-Hagan, Virginia, author. | Bane, Jeff, 1957- illustrator.
Title: Rosalyn Sussman Yalow / by Virginia Loh-Hagan ; illustrator: Jeff Bane.
Other titles: My itty-bitty bio.
Description: Ann Arbor, Michigan : Cherry Lake Publishing, [2018] | Series: My itty-bitty bio | Includes index. | Audience: K to grade 3.
Identifiers: LCCN 2017033455| ISBN 9781534107144 (hardcover) | ISBN 9781534108134 (pbk.) | ISBN 9781534109124 (pdf) | ISBN 9781534120112 (hosted ebook)
Subjects: LCSH: Yalow, Rosalyn S. (Rosalyn Sussman), 1921-2011--Juvenile literature. | Women medical scientists--United States--Biography--Juvenile literature.
Classification: LCC R154.Y24 L64 2018 | DDC 610.92 [B] --dc23
LC record available at https://lccn.loc.gov/2017033455

Printed in the United States of America
Corporate Graphics

table of contents

My Story 4

Timeline .22

Glossary .24

Index 24

About the author: Dr. Virginia Loh-Hagan is an author, university professor, former classroom teacher, and curriculum designer. Like Rosalyn, she believes successful women can have a career and family. She lives in San Diego with her very tall husband and very naughty dogs. To learn more about her, visit: www.virginialoh.com

About the illustrator: Jeff Bane and his two business partners own a studio along the American River in Folsom, California, home of the 1849 Gold Rush. When Jeff's not sketching or illustrating for clients, he's either swimming or kayaking in the river to relax.

I was born in New York. It was 1921.

I read before preschool. I went to the library. I went every week.

Women weren't treated fairly. That didn't stop me.

I finished school. I studied **physics**.

What do you want to study?

I met Dr. Solomon Berson.
We wanted to make sick people better.

People respected him more.
It wasn't right.

How do you help others?

We made a special tool. It let us see tiny things in the body.

This helped doctors. This **cured** people.

I won the Nobel Prize. This award goes to people who do important work.

I was the second American woman to get this.

glossary

cured (KYOORD) made someone who was sick better

inspire (in-SPYR) to fill someone with a feeling or an idea

physics (FIZ-iks) the study of movement, force, light, heat, sound, and electricity

science (SYE-uhns) the study of nature and the world we live in

index

birth, 4

library, 6

Nobel Prize, 18

school, 6, 10, 12
science, 8, 12, 16

war, 10
women, 10, 12, 14, 18, 20